DANNY DRUMM'S HEROES
by
Robert Skimin

FIRST EDITION July 2006
Print Executors Citicap Channels, Ltd., New Delhi, India
www.citibazaar.com / connect@citibazaar.com

Illustrations by Nacho Garcia
Book design by Gabe Quesada
Series Editor, Peg Tremper

Publisher's Cataloging-in-Publication Data
Skimin, Robert
Danny Drumm's Heroes, Volume 2, America's Beginnings—The Spaniards / Robert Skimin
1. History 2. Children's Literature 3. Spanish Colonization 4. Aztecs
5. New Spain 6. Hernan Cortes 7. U.S. Southwest I. Robert Skimin. II. Title

Library of Congress Control Number: 2006930689

ISBN: 0-9769958-5-9

01 02 03 04 05   10 9 8 7 6 5 4 3 2 1

DANNY DRUMM'S HEROES
Volume 2, America's Beginnings—The Spaniards
by
Robert Skimin

Barbed Wire Publishing
Las Cruces, NM
www.barbed-wire.net

Here we are again, Shadow, at the beginning of our country.

Many people think the first people came from Asia, across a thin strip

of land called the Bering Land Bridge up in Alaska, but some of the first

Indians could have come by boat from the Pacific Ocean. It was so long

ago that we'll never know.

Back about 1,000 years ago, the first Europeans

to set foot on North America were some adventurous

Norsemen, or *Vikings*, as they are often called. But since there

were no newspapers, TV, nor radio, the rest of Europe didn't know about it.

About 500 years later, another adventurous seaman named Christopher

Columbus dreamed of sailing west to reach the riches of India. Overcoming

many obstacles, Columbus talked Queen Isabella

of Spain into sponsoring a voyage.

Columbus assembled crews for three small ships, the *Nina*, the *Pinta*, and the *Santa Maria*. He was the captain of the *Santa Maria*. The tiny fleet sailed from Spain in the fall of 1492, and landed some ten weeks later in the West Indies.

You see, Shadow, he thought he was in India, so he called the natives he met "Indians." Later Columbus made three more voyages to the new lands, and this opened up the New World for conquest by the Spaniards.

This place was what became "New Spain" to Spanish settlers seeking fame and riches. Spain was a strongly Catholic country, so religious conversion of the natives was important. Conversion, Shadow, is changing someone's religion.

The Indians in New Spain, which soon became Mexico, worshiped idols and many animal gods. There were many different Indian tribes, and many were enemies of each other.

In 1519, almost thirty years after Columbus, Hernan Cortes led an expedition toward what was to become Mexico City. There, an empire of tribes called the Aztecs was ruled by a rich and powerful tribe called the Mexica (Muh-SHE-kuh). Their king was Montezuma II (Mon-teh-ZOOM-uh), and their capital city was Tenochtitlan (Tay-nohch-TEE-tlan).

The Aztecs believed that a bearded white-skinned god would someday return to rule over them. Cortes and his soldiers wore armor that reflected the sun. They had powerful weapons, and rode animals the Aztecs had never seen—horses. At first, Shadow, the Indians thought that the soldiers on horses were one creature. The Aztecs thought Cortes was the god they were expecting.

Perhaps the most important person Cortes met, Shadow, was a beautiful Indian woman named Marina. She was a linguist—that means she could speak many languages—and she had learned Spanish. She became both his advisor and his link to the many tribes he met on his way.

As he and his tiny army of about 500 Conquistadors (Con-KEE-sta-doors) marched toward Tenochtitlan, Marina translated his Spanish to the local dialects. Dialects are ways of speaking in different places.

But soon he had to pass through the lands of

the ferocious Tlaxcalans (Tuh-lach-KAL-uns).

They had some hard-fought battles, but

Cortes bravely won out and the Tlaxcalans

became his allies against the Aztecs.

Because they thought Cortes was a god, the Aztecs didn't fight very hard to defend their capital of several million people. Montezuma, who lived in a great palace, was taken prisoner when the Spaniards entered the city. Cortes and his men had never seen a city that big or that clean. In fact, Shadow, Tenochtitlan was the biggest city in the world at that time.

Cortes found vast riches and sent many of them back to the
Spanish king in Madrid. There he was hailed as a great hero!
General Narvaez (Nar-vah-ehzzz), a jealous, Spanish rival of
Cortes, was leading his army towards the capital.

Leaving just 200 soldiers in Tenochtitlan, Cortes rushed the rest
of his small army to intercept his rival in the jungle. He bravely
attacked the much larger force at night and captured Narvaez,
then convinced the survivors to join him.

16

When he returned to the Aztec capital, the Indians attacked him, and Montezuma was killed. Again, Cortes defeated them. And many more riches were sent back to the Spanish king.

Cortes was a great hero back in Spain. He was appointed governor and captain general of New Spain. The Aztec capital, which had been badly damaged in the battles, was rebuilt and named Mexico City. Spaniards would control Mexico for 300 years.

Of course the Spanish soldiers and later Spanish settlers married the beautiful Indian girls. Their children were known as *mestizos*, meaning of mixed blood. (Today nearly all Mexicans are mestizos, Shadow.) The people of Spanish blood lived fairly well, but the Indians remained poor.

Mexico was rich in minerals, particularly silver.

The Spaniards developed mines and more cities,

such as Zacatecas (Za-kuh-TAKE-us).

The Spaniards found more than minerals, Shadow.

They also "discovered" tomatoes, corn, squash,

beans, potatoes, avocados, and *chocolate*! Sorry,

Shadow, chocolate is bad for dogs.

The priests who came as missionaries also started churches. They baptized many children and adults as the churches were being built. Sometimes, they taught the kids to read. No, Shadow, they didn't make the dogs into Christians!

At times, the ways of the Spaniards were considered cruel, but the ways of the Aztecs had also been barbaric—that means savage or brutal. When Cortes arrived, the Aztecs were offering human sacrifices to their gods. Most of the victims were slaves or people captured in war. No wonder other tribes didn't like the Aztecs, Shadow.

Spaniards came by the hundreds to New Spain. Kids grew up

speaking Spanish. And as soldiers and settlers arrived, the

country, from the Atlantic Ocean to the Pacific Ocean, became

more and more a colony of old Spain.

But even the gold and silver of New Spain was not enough for the

Spaniards. They heard that the magical and rich Cibola, the Seven

Cities of Gold, were somewhere up in the North. In our next book,

Shadow, we will look for them.

THE END.

25

Other Books You Might Also Enjoy

The Lost Temple of the Aztecs: What it was like when the Spanish invaded Mexico by Shelley Tanaka uses the discovery of the temple in Mexico City to tell the story of the Spanish conquest.

What the Aztecs Told Me by Maria Cristina Urrutia. A sixteenth-century Spanish friar in Mexico tells what he learned from Aztec elders about the language, beliefs, and customs of their land.

Your librarian can help you find more.

Additional Books in This Series

Volume 1, Johnny Clem

Volume 2, America's Beginnings—The Spaniards

Volume 3, New Mexico Settlement

Volume 4, The Pilgrims

Volume 5, British Colonies

Volume 6, Eastern Indians

Volume 7, Slavery in the Colonies

Volume 8, The Pre-Revolutionary Era

Volume 9, Revolutionary War

Subsequent volumes will tell the stories of other
heroes and heroines of the American Experience.